Get In Shape

with Kettlebell Training

The 30 Best Kettlebell Workout Exercises and
Top Sculpting Moves To Lose Weight At Home

Want To Get In Shape Faster?
Add These Books To Your Daily Workout Routine!

Discover Other Great Books By
Julie Schoen

Disclaimer

This book contains general information and is for informational purposes only. You should use proper discretion, and consult with a health care practitioner, before following any of the exercises, techniques, or plans described in this book. The author and publisher expressly disclaim responsibility for any adverse effects that may result from the use or application of the information contained in this book.

Contents:

GET IN SHAPE

"I don't get it," I remember telling my college weight lifting instructor as he tried to convince me that a 10-pound Kettlebell was different than a 10-pound dumbbell. "It's the same weight and I'm still lifting it. Why does it matter that it has a handle and a funky shape?" My instructor smiled, knowing all too well that he knew something I didn't, "You'll see some day."

Lose The Dumb Bells

That some day came three years after my first weight training class when I attended a personal training workshop in San Diego. "Dumbbells are called that for a reason," he yelled at a crowded exercise room of a downtown gym. "Kettlebells, he proclaimed, "Are one of the best ways to effectively train because they are always forcing you to work." Once again, I was dumbfounded.

But then the workout came. A grueling hour-long Kettlebell exclusive workout – the hardest workout I had ever done in my life. And that's saying something. I live for intense workouts. I want more when everyone else is begging for mercy. 5 am run? I'll be there at 4:30 doing sprints. Just finished a 10k? Who's up for kickboxing? 90 minutes of hot yoga? That's my relaxation after a 90-minute soccer game. But an hour of Kettlebells? I'm dead.

Train Like The Soviet Army

Developed in Russia in the 1700's, Kettlebells were used to train the Soviet army through intense physical condition workouts. Kettlebells arrived in the United States in the 1960's, but didn't really start gaining popularity until the 21st century when programs began training fitness instructors and personal trainers in how to exclusively use the cannon ball shaped weights to torture and, more importantly, get amazing results for clients in record time.

Swinging Your Way To Strength

Because of the way Kettlebells are shaped, the weight is distributed disproportionately beyond the hand when it is held, which makes them fantastic for particular movements, such as ballistic and swinging, that normal dumbbells and weights just can't do. Not only will Kettlebells build strength, they are designed to build endurance because reps can be done in a continuous flow without stopping between reps. This means that Kettlebell workouts usually involve more reps than a typical barbell or dumbbell-centered workout.

The handle on the Kettlebell is another reason why working out with it is so much fun (fun might not be the exact word I'm looking for…) because it allows you to rotate your hand, wrist, and arm that tradition weights don't. You'll notice the difference when you discover that Kettlebells can be held with an open hand instead of a tight grip.

In order to move the Kettlebell the body must use several muscles at once, which mimic real-life physical activities (well, real-life if you live on a farm), such as shoveling hay or even roping cattle. This is useful even if you are not planning to work at a dude ranch any time soon. It doesn't take a genius to figure out that working more muscles at once means more calories burnt and incredible (and sexy) results faster than you can say "Turkish Get Up".

Nice Ass, Mobile Body

Beyond the innumerable list of celebrities and models (both male and female) that use Kettlebells to get them photo shoot fresh, it's interesting to note that physical therapists, people interested more in how the body functions than how good your ass looks, love Kettlebells. Why? Because these funky-shaped weights help to improve (or recover) range of motion and flexibility in the body. Unlike bench presses and other gym-centric exercises, Kettlebells allow the body to move.

This is why it's cool that Kettlebell exercises mimic daily farm activities – by working out with movements that are actually useful (if shoveling hay isn't in your daily routine, think about lifting kids, moving furniture, gardening, etc.). And when you strengthen muscles you actually use, your body will thank you by staying healthy and mobile. Throw in Michelle Obama arms, Cameron Diaz legs, and Demi Moore's core, and you now have one thousand and one reasons to start using Kettlebells today.

Sweat, Sweat Baby

So if you are ready for one of the toughest workouts of your life, a killer body, and peace of mind knowing that you'll be able to sweep your floors well into your eighties, then grab your Kettlebells and get ready to sweat like you never have before.

Don't say I didn't warn you.

Love!
Julie

This beautiful greenhouse on an organic farm in New Mexico served as the back-drop for the images in this book (and a shady refuge &from the sun in between takes!)

3 EFFECTIVE WORKOUT PLANS

The beauty of Kettlebells is that you really don't need much time at all to work up a sweat and start reaping the rewards of a sexy, fit, and sculpted body. In ten minutes you can get a better workout and much more flattering results than you could in sixty minutes on a treadmill. Have more time? Get ready to feel the burn and make your body the envy of women everywhere.

The Equipment

No longer just cast-iron globes, Kettlebells come in a wide variety of colors and weights, making them an accessible choice no matter your fitness level. I like to have at least two sets, one much lighter than the other, so that I can perform a variety of exercises at varying intensities. You will want to have at least 2 Kettlebells of the same weight for certain exercises where you will be using a weight in each hand. Most of the time, however, you will just be using one. For most women I recommend getting 2 Kettlebells of a lighter weight that they use most frequently (for me this is the 7-pounders). Then, have on hand at least 1 Kettlebell of a heavier weight for exercises that you want to feel more challenging (I'll go all the way up to a 15-pounder for some).

Kettlebells and the exercises that go along with them are different from other weights. You might be surprised that the weight you use for dumbbells is not the weight you will want for Kettlebells. The best piece of advice I can give you is save your receipts. After going through a few of the workouts, you'll get a good idea if you will want more or less weight. Don't be afraid to go back and get a weight that is ideal for your body. Or, be like me, and start a small Kettlebell collection of varying weights, ready to go at a moment's notice.

Each exercise in this book lists which body parts it targets as well as a "Heavy" or "Light" recommendation. Because preferences and abilities vary greatly, I decided not to list a specific weight – what works for me doesn't always work for my clients and won't necessarily work for you either.

Whatever weight you choose for your reps, be sure that you are not sacrificing form in order to lift a heavier weight. It's much more effective (and safer) to use a weight in which you can complete your reps efficiently and safely while still finding a challenge. Over time the weight you use should increase so that you stay challenged without having to do tons of reps.

10 Minute Workout

Choose 5 of the following Kettlebell exercises. Do each exercise for 1 minute completing as many reps as possible. This is 1 set. Do 2 sets of all of the moves for a total of 2 minutes at each exercise.

If not taking any breaks for 10 minutes straight is tough (and believe me it is!), start by doing 30 seconds of work followed by 30 seconds of rest. As you build endurance and strength you can do 40 seconds work and 20 seconds rest, 50 seconds work and 10 seconds rest, until you are finally at the non-stop 10-minute work out.

20 Minute Workout

Choose 6 of the following Kettlebell exercises. Do 2 sets of each move, 25 reps in each set. Complete 1 set of all of the exercises before starting the second set – be sure to do the exercises in the same order for each set. Try your best to not rest between reps or sets – 20 minutes non-stop! Go!

30 Minute Workout

Begin by doing 5 minutes of cardio, any combination of mountain climbers, squat thrusts, sprints, or jump roping. Then choose 6 of the following Kettlebell exercises. Do each exercise for 60 seconds, completing as many reps as possible – this will equal 1 set. If an exercise requires you to switch sides, switch after 30 seconds. Rest for 1 minute in between exercises. Do 2 sets of each exercise (2 minutes total).

THE 30 BEST KETTLEBELL EXERCISES

1. Russian Swing

Kettlebell Weight: Heavy
Targets: Total Body

Stand with your feet wide and knees bent. Hold the Kettlebell in your hands between your legs, arms straight and back straight. In a quick movement, straighten your legs and simultaneously swing the Kettlebell in front of you until your arms are level with the ground. To perform this exercise properly, make sure you thrust your hips forward as you swing the Kettlebell up. Return to the starting position to complete 1 rep.

Note: The swings should be done consecutively without stopping so that you work with the momentum of the weight. Be careful as to not stop abruptly mid-swing – come to a stop slowly after finishing your reps.

2. One Arm Russian Swing

Kettlebell Weight: Light
Targets: Total Body

Stand with your feet just wider than shoulder width apart, knees slightly bent. Hold the Kettlebell in one hand between your legs, back straight and arm straight. As you swing the Kettlebell up to level with the ground, straighten the legs to stand. Immediately reach for the Kettlebell with the opposite hand and return to the starting position.

Repeat the swing with the opposite hand for the next rep.

Note: The swings should be done consecutively without stopping so that you work with the momentum of the weight. Be careful as to not stop abruptly mid-swing – come to a stop slowly after finishing your reps.

3. American Swing

Kettlebell Weight: Heavy
Targets: Total Body

Stand with your feet wide holding the Kettlebell with both hands in between your legs. Bend your knees slightly, but keep the back straight. Swing the Kettlebell up all the way over your head with straight arms. As you do so, straighten the legs and thrust the hips forward. Keep the heels on the ground the entire time, pushing down into the ground with them for more power.

Return to the starting position to finish 1 rep.

Note: *The swings should be done consecutively without stopping so that you work with the momentum of the weight. Be careful as to not stop abruptly mid-swing – come to a stop slowly after finishing your reps.*

4. Turkish Get Up

Kettlebell Weight: Light (to start – you should progress to heavier weights once you get the hang of the exercise)
Targets: Total Body

Lie down flat on your back. Holding the Kettlebell in your right hand, extend the arm straight up in the air, perpendicular to the ground. Keeping your eye on the Kettlebell, use your left hand, your core, and your legs to help you sit up and then come all the way to stand. Reverse the process to lie down to finish 1 rep.

For your next rep, change hands and work the other side.

The key to doing this exercise is making sure that the arm stays straight and the Kettlebell stays over your head the entire time. Start slow and with lightweight Kettlebells, working to get faster with heavier weights the more you practice.

5. Warrior Row

Kettlebell Weight: Light
Targets: Triceps, Back, Legs, and Glutes

Stand with your feet hip-width apart. Hold the Kettlebell in your left hand. Shift your weight into the right leg and lift the left off the ground. Bend the left elbow until the upper arm is level with the ground, performing a row. Try to keep the upper body and lifted leg in one line as much as possible. Return to the starting position to finish one rep.

Do all of your reps on 1 side before switching sides to complete the set.

6. Triangle Down and Up

Kettlebell Weight: Light
Targets: Shoulders, Back, Core, Glutes, and Legs

Stand with your feet slightly wider than shoulder-width apart. Hold the Kettlebell in your right hand. Extend the arm straight over your head, bicep near your ear and palm facing away from you. Keeping your gaze at the Kettlebell, start to slide your left hand down your left leg until it reaches your foot. All the while, keep the right arm straight and over your head with your eyes focused.

Slowly bring yourself back to stand to finish 1 rep. In between reps, keep the Kettlebell over your head. Do all of your reps on one side before switching sides to finish the set.

7. Water Carry

Kettlebell Weight: Heavy
Targets: Total Body

Stand with a Kettlebell in each hand. Begin to walk forward. As you step the right foot forward raise the right arm straight over your head, rotating the palm of your hand so that it faces away from you. As you step forward with the left foot, lower the right arm and raise the left. This is 1 rep.

Pick up the pace to make this exercise more challenging. Instead of counting reps, you can also work for a set amount of time, moving as quickly as possible.

8. Pick Up Press

Kettlebell Weight: Light
Targets: Legs, Glutes, Shoulders, and Back

Stand with your feet hip-width apart. Hold the Kettlebell in your right hand, palm facing the body. Your left arm should extend away from your body, palm down. Bend your knees and come into a squat. Keep the back straight. As you straighten your legs lift the Kettlebell straight over your head – don't bend the elbow. Return to the starting position to finish 1 rep.

Do all of your reps on 1 side before switching sides to finish the set.

9. Robin Hood

Kettlebell Weight: Light
Targets: Shoulders, Biceps, Back, Glutes, and Legs

Stagger your feet so that the left foot is a few feet in front of the right. Hold a Kettlebell in each hand. Bend both of your knees and twist to the left, bringing the right hand to the left foot. As you straighten your legs, bend the right elbow and bring the Kettlebell to your right hip. This is 1 rep.

Do all of your reps on 1 side before switching sides to finish the set.

10. Swing Thru Lunge Press

Kettlebell Weight: Light
Targets: Shoulders, Biceps, Core, Glutes, and Legs

Hold a Kettlebell in each hand. Stand with your feet hip-width apart. Bend your elbows to bring the Kettlebells by your shoulders, palms facing towards the body. Step forward with the right leg to come into a lunge. The right thigh should be level with the ground and the knee over the ankle. Straighten your right leg as you swing your left leg in front of you, balancing on one leg. Simultaneously, straighten the arms over your head, rotating the arms so that the palms face away from your body.

Swing the left leg back into the lunge to finish 1 rep. Half way through your reps, switch legs so that your left leg is forward in the lunge.

11. Michael Jordan Lunge

Kettlebell Weight: Heavy
Targets: Triceps, Glutes, and Legs

Stand with your feet staggered, right foot in front of left with the Kettlebell in your right hand. Come into a lunge position, bending both knees and keeping the right knee behind the right toes. Pass the Kettlebell under the right leg to the left hand and press up to stand.

For the next rep, step back with the right leg into a lunge and pass the Kettlebell under the left leg to the right hand.

Do the reps continuously without stopping for the entire set.

12. Biceps To Triceps

Kettlebell Weight: Light
Targets: Shoulders, Biceps, and Triceps

Stand with your feet hip-width apart. Hold the Kettlebell with your left hand, palm facing away from your body. Bend the elbow and bring your left hand to your shoulder, like a biceps curl. Then straighten the arm to bring the weight over the head, palm of the hand faces behind you. Bend the elbow again to lower the weight behind your head, working your triceps. As you do this make sure the elbow stays next to the head. Return to the starting position slowly to finish 1 rep.

Do all of your reps on one side before switching sides to complete the set.

13. Winner's Squat

Kettlebell Weight: Light
Targets: Glutes, Legs, Biceps, Triceps, and Shoulders

Stand with your feet wide, toes pointing out at a 45-degree angle. Hold a Kettlebell in each hand. Bend your elbows and bring your hands to your shoulders, palms facing your body. Bend your knees and come into a wide squat, weight in your heels and knees behind your toes. As you squat, extend your arms straight out to the sides at a 45-degree angle, making a capital "V". Rotate your arms so that your palms face away from your body.

Return to the starting position to finish 1 rep.

14. Dancer's Lunge

Kettlebell Weight: Light
Targets: Shoulders, Biceps, Glutes, and Legs

Stand with your feet wide. Hold a Kettlebell in each hand. Raise your arms so that they are level with the ground, palms face down. Step the right leg behind the left, bending both knees to come into a cross-legged squat. As you do so pull your elbows in towards your ribs, rotating the palms of the hands so they face up.

Return to the starting position and repeat on the other side to complete 1 rep.

15. Chest Press Sit Up

Kettlebell Weight: Light
Targets: Triceps, Chest, and Core

Lie down flat on your back with the Kettlebell in your left hand and knees bent. Bend the left elbow, palm facing away from your body and upper arm resting on the ground. Place your right hand on the ground alongside your body, palm facing down. Press the Kettlebell up above the body with the left arm until it is straight. Then, using your core and your right hand, press yourself up to sit, keeping the left arm straight and the Kettlebell above your head. Lower back down to the starting position to finish the rep. Do half of the reps on 1 side before switching sides and finishing the second half on the other.

The trick to this exercise is using your free hand as a support arm to help propel you up. As you sit up, bring the free hand behind you, palm facing down and fingers pointing away from the body, so that you have more momentum to sit up quickly.

16. 3-Point Press (Insert Images 1 and 2)

Kettlebell Weight: Light
Targets: Shoulders, Back, and Chest

Stand with your feet together. Place a Kettlebell in each hand, elbows bent and palms facing your body. Lift your elbows until your triceps are level with the ground and your forearms perpendicular. Keeping your arms at this level, move the elbows to the sides, creating "goalpost" arms. Then, press the weights up, extending your arms straight, palms facing away from your body.

Return to the starting position slowly to finish 1 rep.

17. Self Defense Figure 8

Kettlebell Weight: Heavy
Targets: Shoulders, Back, Core, Glutes, and Legs

Stand with your feet wide and the Kettlebell in your right hand. Bend your knees to squat and swing the Kettlebell between your legs, passing it behind the left leg and grabbing it with your left hand. Swing the Kettlebell up with your left arm, holding the bottom of the weight with your right hand. In this position, the left elbow should be in line with the shoulder and the forearm parallel with the ground.

Then, twist to the right, quickly moving the left elbow across the body as if you were using it to punch someone. Lower the weight back down with the left arm and pass it through the legs to the other side.

This is 1 rep. Repeat the same actions on the other side.

18. High Kick Farmer

Kettlebell Weight: Heavy
Targets: Total Body

Hold a Kettlebell in each hand. Begin to walk forward, kicking one leg at a time straight up and as high as you can. Keep the back straight as you do so. If space allows, move forward as you walk. If you don't have much space, simply swing your leg up and back down to the starting position; then switch legs to finish the rep.

This exercise can be done for time rather than reps to increase intensity and to encourage you to move as quickly as possible.

19. Hot Potato

Kettlebell Weight: Heavy
Targets: Biceps, Triceps, Shoulders, Core, Glutes, and Legs

Hold the Kettlebell straight out in front of you, arms level with the ground. With your feet hip-width apart, bend your knees and squat. Be sure that you keep the back straight and the knees behind the toes as you do so. Staying low in the squat, start to walk forward. Continue to hold the weight straight out in front of you.

A step forward with each foot counts as 1 rep. Or perform this exercise for time rather than reps to increase the intensity.

20. Lumberjack

Kettlebell Weight: Light
Targets: Legs, Glutes, Shoulders, Triceps, Biceps, and Core

Hold the Kettlebell with both hands, palms facing away from your body. Stagger your feet so that the right foot is about 2 feet in front of the left. With the knees slightly bent, lift the Kettlebell over your right shoulder, palms facing behind your body and backs of the arms level with the ground. As you bring the Kettlebell to your left hip, bend both knees to come into a lunge. The right thigh should be level with the ground. Return to the starting position to finish 1 rep.

Do all of your reps on 1 side before switching sides to complete the set.

21. Squat Thrust Pick-Ups

Kettlebell Weight: Heavy
Targets: Legs, Glutes, Triceps, Biceps, and Shoulders

Squat down with your hands on the handles of the Kettlebells, feet hip-width apart. Your hands should be directly under your shoulders. Look forward as you hop your feet back to come into a plank position. Hold the plank momentarily so that the core starts to engage. Then, jump forward, keeping your hands on the Kettlebells as you do so.

Straighten the legs and pick the weights up, bending the elbows so that the palms face the body. Immediately press the arms straight over your hand, rotating the arms so that the palms face away from the body.

Return to the starting position to finish 1 rep.

Note: If it is too difficult to hop back into the Plank position holding onto the handles of the Kettlebell, move your hands so that they are under the handle on top of the weight.

22. Weighted One-Leg Lift

Kettlebell Weight: Heavy
Targets: Back, Shoulders, Glutes, Core, and Legs

Hold the Kettlebell with both hands. Stand with your feet hip-width apart. Shift your weight into the right leg. Lift your left leg off the ground, extending it behind you. As you lift the left leg, lower your torso so that the Kettlebell is just a few inches off the ground. Bend the left knee and bring it towards the back of the right leg. As you do so, try to keep the left foot as high off the ground as possible.

Return to the starting position to finish 1 rep. Do all of your reps with one leg before switching legs to finish the set.

23. Mia Hamm Feet

Kettlebell Weight: Light or Heavy
Targets: Core, Glutes, and Legs

Set the Kettlebell on its side on the ground so the handle is resting flat. Pumping your arms rapidly, begin to tap the Kettlebell with your feet, running in place as quickly as possible. Tap the Kettlebell with the right foot and then the left to complete 1 rep.

This exercise can be done for time too in order to increase intensity (and heart rate!)

24. Arnold Lunge

Kettlebell Weight: Light
Targets: Biceps, Shoulders, Glutes, and Legs

Hold a Kettlebell in each hand, palms facing away from the body. Step the right foot forward and come into a lunge position, bending both knees so that the right thigh is parallel with the ground. Staying in the lunge position, bend the elbows to perform a biceps curl. Then, rotate the palms forward and press the arms straight over the head. Lower the arms back to the starting position to finish 1 rep.

Alternate the leg that is forward in the lunge after doing each rep.

25. Double Edge Reach

Kettlebell Weight: Light
Targets: Shoulders, Triceps, Back, Core, Glutes, and Legs

Stand with you feet shoulder-width apart. Hold a Kettlebell in each hand. Bend to the right as you extend your left arm straight over your head, reaching as far as you can to the left, bicep right by the ear. As you do so, take the right arm straight behind you, palm facing up, reaching past the left hip if possible. Return to the starting position and repeat on the other side to finish 1 rep.

26. Extended One-Leg Touch

Kettlebell Weight: Heavy
Targets: Glutes and Legs

Stand with the Kettlebell in your right hand, right foot slightly behind the left. Place your left hand on your hip. With a small bend in the left knee, lift the right leg off the ground and lower the Kettlebell until it almost touches. Keep the back straight. Return to the starting position to finish 1 rep.

Do all of your reps on 1 side before switching sides to finish the set.

27. Push Up Row

Kettlebell Weight: Heavy
Targets: Triceps, Shoulders, Chest, Back, Core

Come to the top of a pushup with both hands on the handles of the Kettlebells. Place your hands directly under your shoulders. Move your feet apart, slightly wider than your hips, to help stabilize your body as you work. With the body in one straight line, bend the elbows and come into a pushup – keep the elbows close to the body as you do so.

After completing the pushup, lift the Kettlebell in your left hand off the ground to perform a row, rotating the body to the right side. Lower the left hand back to the ground to the starting position.

Switch the side you row on after each rep, not forgetting to do a push up in between each!

28. Squat Row

Kettlebell Weight: Heavy
Targets: Biceps, Back, and Core

Stand with your feet hip width apart. Hold the Kettlebell with both of your hands, arms straight and palms facing the body. Come into a squat position, keeping the weight in your heels and your knees behind your toes. Lift your hands to your chest, extending the elbows out to the sides. As you do, be sure that you keep the back as straight as possible.

To finish the rep, bring your arms back to the starting position. Stay in the squat position between reps.

29. Power Press

Kettlebell Weight: Heavy
Targets: Shoulders, Triceps, Glutes, and Legs

Stand with feet wide and the Kettlebell in your right hand. Bend your right elbow and bring the Kettlebell to your right shoulder, palm facing your body. Bend your knees and come into a squat position, making sure the weight stays in your heels and your back is straight. As you straighten your legs, quickly lift the right arm over your head, rotating the palm so it now faces away from your body. Return to the starting position to finish 1 rep.

Do all of your reps on 1 side before switching sides to finish the set.

30. Plank Row Pass

Kettlebell Weight: Heavy
Targets: Triceps, Shoulders, Back, and Core

Come into a plank position with the right hand holding the handle of the Kettlebell and your left hand on the ground. Make sure your body is level with the ground and your hands are under your shoulders. Spread the feet apart, slightly wider than the hips, for extra stability. Keeping the right elbow in close to the body, lift the Kettlebell off the ground to perform a row. Lower the Kettlebell back to the ground to finish 1 rep.

Grab onto the handle with the left hand, placing the right hand on the ground, and repeat on the other side for the next rep.

EXERCISE INDEX

Triceps

- High Kick Farmer
- Water Carry
- Power Press
- Squat Thrust Pick-Ups
- Lumberjack
- Hot Potato
- Biceps To Triceps
- Warrior Row
- Double Edge Reach
- Russian Swing
- American Swing
- Michael Jordan Lunge
- Plank Row Pass
- Chest Press Sit Up
- One Arm Russian Swing
- Push Up Row
- Turkish Get Up

Biceps

- Arnold Lunge
- Winner's Squat
- Squat Row
- High Kick Farmer
- Water Carry
- Squat Thrust Pick-Ups
- Lumberjack
- Hot Potato
- Biceps To Triceps

- Swing Thru Lunge Press
- Dancer's Lunge
- Robin Hood
- Russian Swing
- American Swing
- One Arm Russian Swing
- Turkish Get Up

Shoulders

- Pick Up Press
- Arnold Lunge
- 3-Point Press
- Winner's Squat
- Triangle Down and Up
- High Kick Farmer
- Water Carry
- Power Press
- Squat Thrust Pick-Ups
- Lumberjack
- Hot Potato
- Biceps To Triceps
- Swing Thru Lunge Press
- Weighted One-Leg Lift
- Dancer's Lunge
- Double Edge Reach
- Robin Hood
- Russian Swing
- American Swing
- Plank Row Pass
- Self Defense Figure 8

- One Arm Russian Swing
- Push Up Row
- Turkish Get Up

Chest

- 3-Point Press
- High Kick Farmer
- Water Carry
- Russian Swing
- American Swing
- Chest Press Sit Up
- One Arm Russian Swing
- Push Up Row
- Turkish Get Up

Back

- Pick Up Press
- 3-Point Press
- Triangle Down and Up
- Squat Row
- High Kick Farmer
- Water Carry
- Warrior Row
- Weighted One-Leg Lift
- Double Edge Reach
- Robin Hood
- Russian Swing
- American Swing
- Plank Row Pass
- Self Defense Figure 8
- One Arm Russian Swing
- Push Up Row
- Turkish Get Up

Core

- High Kick Farmer
- Water Carry

- Lumberjack
- Hot Potato
- Triangle Down and Up
- Swing Thru Lunge Press
- Weighted One-Leg Lift
- Double Edge Reach
- Russian Swing
- American Swing
- Plank Row Pass
- Self Defense Figure 8
- Chest Press Sit Up
- Mia Hamm Feet
- One Arm Russian Swing
- Push Up Row
- Turkish Get Up

Glutes

- Pick Up Press
- Arnold Lunge
- Winner's Squat
- Triangle Down and Up
- High Kick Farmer
- Water Carry
- Power Press
- Squat Thrust Pick-Ups
- Lumberjack
- Extended One-Leg Touch
- Hot Potato
- Warrior Row
- Swing Thru Lunge Press
- Weighted One-Leg Lift
- Dancer's Lunge
- Double Edge Reach
- Robin Hood
- Russian Swing
- American Swing
- Michael Jordan Lunge
- Self Defense Figure 8

- Mia Hamm Feet
- One Arm Russian Swing
- Turkish Get Up

Legs

- Pick Up Press
- Arnold Lunge
- Winner's Squat
- Triangle Down and Up
- High Kick Farmer
- Water Carry
- Power Press
- Squat Thrust Pick-Ups
- Lumberjack
- Extended One-Leg Touch

- Hot Potato
- Warrior Row
- Swing Thru Lunge Press
- Weighted One-Leg Lift
- Dancer's Lunge
- Double Edge Reach
- Robin Hood
- Russian Swing
- American Swing
- Michael Jordan Lunge
- Self Defense Figure 8
- Mia Hamm Feet
- One Arm Russian Swing
- Turkish Get Up

BONUS WORKOUT SOUNDTRACKS

Ready to pump up the jams?
Discover great soundtracks for your workouts by visiting the link below:

www.littlepearlpublishing.com/workoutjams

Discover More Great Books At

www.littlepearlpublishing.com

Printed in Great Britain
by Amazon

16885140R00029